LAMENT OF AN AUDIENCE
ON THE DEATH OF AN ARTIST (1985)

Lament of an Audience on the Death of an Artist (1985)

CORDELL STRUG

WIPF & STOCK · Eugene, Oregon

Resource Publications
A division of Wipf and Stock Publishers
199 W 8th Ave, Suite 3
Eugene, OR 97401

Lament of an Audience on the Death of an Artist
(1985)
By Strug, Cordell
Copyright©2008 by Strug, Cordell
ISBN 13: 978-1-5326-8842-3
Publication date 4/12/2019
Previously published by Ytterli Press, 2008

PREFACE (2008)

When Sam Peckinpah died in 1984, I spent some time working out my responses to his work as a whole and, more generally, puzzling over the experience of following contemporary artists as their work takes shape. I ended up lamenting Peckinpah's death, pondering those wonderful movies, and reflecting on what all our watching, reading and listening amounts to in our living. I set it all down in 1985 and put it on a shelf. I think it was supposed to become part of something I can no longer remember.

Looking at it again, after all these years, I thought I might send it forth on its own. It appears pretty much without revision, as its value is of its time. But its judgements are also of its time, and I would judge differently today. I would no longer, for example, consider Steven Spielberg a brainless child, and, after the Bush years, I would be forced to adopt a new standard for the distance between appearance and reality in America.

—C. S.

There was always a bottle present, so that it would seem to him that those fine fierce instants of heart and brain and courage and wiliness and speed were concentrated and distilled into that brown liquor which not women, not boys and children, but only hunters drank, drinking not of the blood they spilled but some condensation of the wild immortal spirit...

—Faulkner, "The Bear"

My heritage has become to me like a lion
    in the forest,
She has lifted up her voice against me;
    therefore I hate her.
Is my heritage to me like a speckled
    bird of prey?
Are the birds of prey against her
    round about?
Go, assemble all the wild beasts;
    bring them to devour.
Many shepherds have destroyed my vineyard,
    they have trampled down my portion,
They have made my pleasant portion
    a desolate wilderness.
They have made it a desolation;
    desolate, it mourns to me.
The whole land is made desolate,
    but no man lays it to heart.

—Jeremiah 12:8-11

The real war poets are always war poets, peace or any-time.

—Randall Jarrell

We learn to read and the world is never the same. Once we were only hands and feet, mouths and eyes, our limits and the world's pressure bound fast to our senses. But, reading, we become like gods, reaching across great distances through signs, so that a person walking toward us will strike us with less of an impact than the words "Americans massacred" glimpsed in a newspaper, less of an impact than the death of Ahab. The shape of our lives cannot be traced without that ability. Reading becomes part of what we do, what we are.

So does watching. Imagine a world without dance or sport or the random, graceful gesture of self-display. Imagine us all clumsy, all incapable of having our attention gripped by a swift and stunning motion. Men and women of skill and passion would never leap before us. We would never see them and our hearts would never leap with them. Such things are as much a part of us as the food we eat, the work we do, the moment of history we inhabit.

Imagine a world without music. Not deafness, but a world of talk, motors, wind, collisions, only without music. Imagine a world without the still and piercing images of the great painters. We would hear and see but we would not hear and see as we do now.

These forms, when they touch us (and not all do and perhaps we hardly understand why some do), mark and define us as deeply as our friends, our enemies, our religions, and our governments. I find biographies incomplete if they don't tell me what someone read, listened to, found beautiful or moving.

Imagine a world without movies.

I know some people can do this, but I can't. Movies have been such a common and crucial part of my life that I can as easily imagine the world without color as without movies. (Perhaps more easily: it would be like an old movie.) When I'm reading nineteenth-century novels, making adjustments for the nonintrusion of the telephone, the necessity of riding horses, the difficulty of getting a divorce, something in me still assumes that some of those long evenings are being spent at the movies. In some foggy corner of my mind, I assume the authors are simply not mentioning the movies, as they aren't mentioning trips to the bathroom. And when I tell myself that of course those who lived before my time didn't go to the movies, then I see in their days a dark gap, about two hours long, joyless and lifeless, at best a coma, at worst suicidal despair.

My life, without the movies I have watched, would be as impoverished as it would be without the people I have known.

'Art and Life', something we used to discuss in philosophy classes, is a ridiculous phrase. What is this 'life' apart from art?

And yet there is something to those images, words, tones, and shapes we call art that sets them apart from (and above) the rest of what we do and are. And there is something that sets apart the artists that create them. Rembrandt and Eakins, making thought perceptible, have deepened the rest of my life. Dickens, Beckett, and Roth, hysterically funny and coldly perceptive, have unsettled everything around me.

Great artists are brilliant people we are privileged to meet through their creations. Drawn in by one or two meetings, we put their lives together for ourselves. Yet it isn't their lives we assemble, but the ideal pilgrimage of their works. Following their paths, we shape our own, even if we're not aware of it.

In this strange way, artists become dear to us. They themselves take on an importance different from the importance of beautiful movements, melodies, harmonies, shapes, and stories and different also from our loved ones. Special people, whom we might find intolerable in person, they seduce us by (and only in) their art. We yearn not for another moment with them but for another creation. Yet not just another creation, but another creation *from them*.

And, like people who are already brilliant and scarred and heavy with experience before we meet them, the artists of the world take shape for us in a disjointed way. We may meet them only by chance or, deliberately, by being guided to their masterpieces. Then we go looking for the rest of them, in libraries, museums, rerun theaters, concert halls, bookstores, and amateur productions. They are always one step ahead of us. We are always assembling them, putting their journeys together in more or less random ways. And we are helped by the studies that others have made of them and the intangible effect they have had on artists who followed them. We can never read Eliot or Pound with quite the incomprehension of an earlier generation. We can never hear the cacophony others heard in Debussy or Stravinsky, grasp the outrage evoked by Manet or Cézanne. Mastering Joyce and Proust, we wonder at the difficulty critics found in *The Sound and the Fury*.

The older artists are there before us, more or less accessible, somewhat easier for us to grasp, yet somewhat more difficult for us to grow with, needing a leap of imagination not only to follow their spirits but also to enter their times.

It is different with artists who are roughly our contemporaries, or whose works are forged and unfold for us through our own time. We may have to struggle even harder to get a view of them. It may still take the masterpiece to call them to our attention. But they bear part of our future with them. Once grasped by them, we wait to have our future enlightened by them. We grope along with them, sometimes parting ways, sometimes waiting breathless for the next creation. We have no way of knowing what lies ahead, not for us and so not for them, not for them and so not for us. We have no way of distinguishing high achievement from low. The studies aren't written yet. Only our own sensibilities and responses guide us.

For me, a prime example of such an artist in literature is Philip Roth. I read *Goodbye, Columbus* in college when I was trying to fight my way out of the Midwestern Polish Catholic world I was born into, and I await each new book by Roth as I might the next reflective look in the mirror. There are books by others that I value more, there are older writers I value more, there are other writers I followed, then dropped and who are perhaps awaiting me around some unforeseeable curve of the future. But this is someone who was writing in my time, of my time, at whose words I thought "yes, this is just right," whose name I searched for when new books were announced.

Ah, but then there were the movies.

Movies, for me at least, were not an acquired taste. No one had to lead me to them or teach me how to appreciate them. My first memories are of sitting in my crib, staring at the television, my first babysitter, mentor, and friend. And I had the great good fortune to see—even before I could spell my own name, choose my own breakfast food, leave my own block, or meet people I wasn't related to—the Hollywood movies of the thirties and forties. The first human beings I knew and loved as an equal, that I laughed and cried with, struggled, won, and lost with were James Cagney, Humphrey Bogart, Pat O'Brien, Errol Flynn, Olivia de Havilland, William Powell, Myrna Loy, Jean Arthur, and so many other beautiful and wonderful actors.

When I was old enough to be taken to movies, they were still the great popular entertainment they had been for three decades and I couldn't have imagined that one day people would rather stay home to watch television (which I looked upon as a small movie museum) than go out to a movie. But the times were changing, even as my family still journeyed to the Chicago Loop to watch the first run of the latest, certain to be enjoyed, John Ford movie.

Not that I could have identified Ford at the time, behind the images of *The Quiet Man*, *Wings of Eagles*, or *Gideon of Scotland Yard*. As most others, we were more likely to follow actors than directors. Still, it did not take the *auteur* theory to tell me that in some products of the great studios one could trace an individual sensibility at work. It hardly took a genius to group the movies of Ford together, even without knowing what a director was, or the movies of Huston, or of Billy Wilder.

For a while, carried away with this theory, I tried to do this with all directors, something which is obvious nonsense. Yet the rejection of it in all cases is equal nonsense.

By the time I was in high school, I had begun to be dimly aware of the fact that movies were not to be taken for granted as facts of life but were in fact artistic creations, that a series of movies by the same director had the grip on me that they did because in them was embodied an artistic pilgrimage, as surely as in a series of novels or plays by the same author—just as compelling, just as worthy of attention. Partially aided by television reruns, I had been primed for this discovery by Huston, Welles,

Ford (and the spectacles of David Lean). But I think it was when I saw Wilder's *Sunset Boulevard* at my high school (a boarding school that showed Saturday night movies to pacify us) that it finally dawned on me that there were identifiable minds at work behind these things I'd watched all my life and that the bitter humor and irony of someone like Wilder, working in a form which was supposed to be *entertaining*, could actually crystallize for me things I was either feeling or groping for, things I needed. (Thus I also realized, in a way teachers could never communicate, that art was real—that the struggle to appreciate Keats or Dickens was worth it because that was what they gave you, too, and that—what a pitiful revelation to a coarse child of the twentieth century—Keats and Dickens didn't last because they were highbrow or because some god of a critic honored them with a gold medal but because they had produced living art, as captivating as the movies.)

Now, why one artist grips you rather than another is a difficult question. Some of them are idiomatic, in the sense that regional turns of phrase are, so that they are familiar and natural to adopt. They are simply around a certain place and time, as we are, and there is an unreflective connection between us.

But all these stories and images and harmonies that seem to come from and deal with other worlds, why should we find them compelling? In a way, the question touches on the nature of imaginative life itself, the nature of contemplation. It certainly isn't a bare interest in the world around us that drives us to one artistic sensibility rather than another. Stories and images about other lives give something important to our lives. They fascinate us, and certain artists fascinate us, because they answer a yearning in us; and what part of nature, of our time or of our own peculiar destiny they speak to is a knot hopeless to unravel.

A work of art is a gift of clarity, one finished, enclosed thing that clarifies both itself and something in us. Gripped by it, we are given a governing image, as it were, to order the messy lives we lead. To ask why this happens is to touch the mystery of language, gesture, communication, and of love, obsession, hope. Those parts of our lives we call art help us read, know, and illuminate those parts of our lives we call life.

To take a religious example: the crucifixion is something so unique, both in its human particulars and its theological interpretations, that it's arguably unrelated to anything else whatsoever. Yet for centuries, it's served as a governing image of human devotion, endurance, suffering, sacrifice: bear a cross, be crucified.

And so particular works become our partners in dialogue. And particular artists become greater partners. When they are thriving as our contemporaries, they are irreplaceable elements of our lives. We meditate, expand, contract, rage, and hope with them, through years that we need no critical apparatus to enter. They have parts of our spirit in their keeping.

But, of course, like parents and older friends, they are not exactly our contemporaries. They are at first mostly older, perhaps less lucky, perhaps more self-destructive than we are. Those we grow up honoring, in the ordinary run of things will burn out or they will die, leaving us alone with their works, our shared pasts, but no real future to speak of.

Sometimes this scarcely matters. By the time Ford and Welles died, the conversation had already ceased, in one case through age, in the other through defeat. But Robert Lowell's death, John Berryman's death, these were endings that brought emptiness with them. I can remember exactly where I was when Hemingway died, too young to have read much of him, young enough to imagine he would always be producing books; I can still hear my father scoffing at the idea that Hemingway could possibly shoot himself *by accident*, as our car radio announced. And I remember the immense feeling of loss when I learned of the deaths of Edmund Wilson and Georg Lukacs, two critics as important to me as any creative artists had been (perhaps because, during the sixties and seventies, when my ignorant contemporaries were ridiculing art and thought, all the immense labor of culture, these two writers were demonstrating for me the value of these things).

The death of an artist, especially an active artist, especially an artist we have grown with, is a terrible loss. In one sense, there is no grief as we usually experience grief at the death of those close to us. In another sense, there is an emptiness equal to or greater than the loss of a loved one.

The death of an artist is the loss of a future, the future as it might have been. We have lost a wise counselor or a court fool whose gross truth will no longer be told. As with all death that strikes near, we die too.

Modern counseling is fond of talking of the redefinition of the self that takes place in recovering from grief. There is certainly some truth in this, but it smacks a little of the mechanical tinkering we try to impose on spiritual problems. It's only another clinical euphemism for bearing the emptiness of death, the emptiness of the dead one, the emptiness of ourselves.

An artist dies and part of us is gone forever—not the past, but the future. We will never be quite what we might have been because we will never hear or see or reflect on what we might have. We are still here but the artist that taught, delighted, shaped, and led us is not.

One died last year who had done this for me and whose

death has provoked these thoughts. He was someone whose works I had sought out for nearly twenty years, so that waiting for the next creation had become an unshakable habit. He had entranced me as no other living artist had ever done. He left me panting for the next work, the next step, the next turn. And I had, sometimes, really to seek out those works, an odd situation since he was an artist not at all esoteric. But the advertising and distribution of his movies were beneath contempt. Yet I managed to find almost all of them, finally, eventually, and looking forward to his new films was like holding on to a lifeline of creative power through these last two decades. But he died last year, in the last month of 1984, when one of the most laughable productions of Hollywood was serving as president of the country, and the difference between appearance and reality in America was at an all-time high, as though he did not have the stomach to see what lay beyond the year whose numbers have come to stand for the death of truth, imagination, and love. I'm still here, but Sam Peckinpah is not.

His passing was marked in a suitable way, befitting both his nature and the universe explored in his work. Friends and longtime admirers grieved, meetings were held, articles and memoirs published—but they were all of the shaggy, personal sort, appearing somewhat on the outskirts, the borders, of both official sanction and popular esteem. Peckinpah was mourned by his own, as was fitting. Inconceivable that he would be referred to as "the late distinguished film director," since that usually implies impeccable grooming, clean hands, and a fossilized talent. Quite in order that the brainless child Spielberg, handing out this year's meaningless Academy Award for direction, should pause to note the passing of François Truffaut and never mention Peckinpah. Truffaut, with his classical profile, his distance from our society, his gentleness, his lightness of touch, falls well within the boundaries of the easily honored. Honoring him we seem to honor ourselves for possessing qualities which in fact have nothing to do with us. On the other hand, those works we ignore at ceremonial times we lump together mindlessly as empty frolics or mechanical horror. We have no room for the art of passion, rage, disgust, and alienation, the art that tears the veil from ourselves and our social arrangements. Of course, this is proper: for an academy to honor such art would be an act of hypocrisy. Spielberg, if it had occurred to him to mention Peckinpah, would probably have been frightened to conjure up such a spectre of wrath.

Of course, it is not unusual for the proper valuation of artists, even great artists, to be slow in coming. Of course, Peckinpah worked, for the most part, in genres that have no value in the eyes of many. (But was it that hard to see he transcended them?) Of course, much of his work was violent and, more to the point surely, much of it drew on savage emotions and agonizing traps. He never warmed the cockles of anyone's heart. And, of course, his own personality and adventures, like Hemingway's, tended to obscure the purity and value of his works.

But, come, was it that difficult to look at a series of films like *Ride the High Country, The Wild Bunch, The Ballad of Cable Hogue, Straw Dogs,* and *Junior Bonner* and see that here was a magnificent achievement of technical mastery and thematic exploration rare in any art? Add to those the mixed achievement of *Major Dundee,* and the beautiful, truncated *Pat Garrett and Billy the Kid* (whose conception, if it had been allowed execution, would have made most films of its era seem simple-minded) and the unusual *Cross of Iron,* so harsh and bitter and ironic (with a sometimes weak script from a sometimes too romantic novel but whose filming and editing is complex and amazing), and the strange, jagged modern trilogy of manipulation, revenge, alienation, and desperate honor—*Bring Me the Head of Alfredo Garcia, The Killer Elite,* and *The Osterman Weekend*—and, allowing for any amount of personal preference and bad publicity and critical obtuseness, it becomes a mystery beyond solution and a truth to oppress the spirit that such an artist was so little valued, so often dismissed.

But if our society desires a black-and-white world of simple problems and happy endings in politics, it is too much to expect that it would seek or discover anything more in art. Scholars I have known have found it surprising that I could value an artist who was so 'primitive', so unintellectual. Pacifists I have known shook their heads at his violence. Women disliked his treatment of women. And I found myself defending these movies and even wondering about myself at times, approaching them in the middle seventies with, as the saying goes, guilty pleasure. But this was silly. The art is undeniable. Moreover, in these movies, there was life, not as we wanted it to be, but as it was.

The key, I think, is that Peckinpah was neither a cultural optimist nor a primitive romantic. He had no faith in social arrangements and none in stripping them away either. He saw the ambiguity of civilization, the greed and hatred and hypocrisy behind it. And he saw the ambiguity of the human heart, the savagery that lay in it, alongside the generosity. His temperament was actually closest to religious figures like Augustine, Luther, Kierkegaard, and Barth. He saw the values of life, its grace, charity, loyalty, as things that had to be learned and fought for, things that sometimes required death from you, receiving it or giving it, things that never came to you purely, but always alloyed with baser things. Thus he could show the disgust and humiliation of trapped loyalty and compromised love. And he could show the ecstasy of violent release. These are things we would rather not see because we would rather not believe they exist.

I have often asked myself how I came to be drawn so strongly to this particular artist, and I think this pitiless view of life (which did not preclude pity or compassion for those trapped in it) was a great part of the attraction. Essential to this view, of course, were the shifting perspectives, the broad sympathies, the presence of contradiction, rage, disgust, sacrifice—all rooted in the lives of recognizable people, not cartoons. Unlikely as this might seem, I saw in Peckinpah in the sixties and seventies something I also saw in Thomas Mann: here was a passionate, stylized art, born out of the energy of a popular art form, which presented a passionate and complex exploration of living issues.

I was ready for something like this when I first saw *Major Dundee*. I was in college at the time, being swept up in the wave of film studies, becoming friends with the kind of people who clap when the names of certain cinematographers appear in the credits, so I was already acquiring the habit of paying attention to who did what in the film I was watching. And I had not been wholly poisoned by the fashion of dismissing everything that came from Hollywood. Some of my friends watched Bergman movies the way they read the editorial page of the *New York Times*. When they swooned over Eisenstein's *Alexander Nevsky*, I was at a loss to see the difference from John Ford. So I went to *Major Dundee* because I went to almost everything that came to town and also because I loved Westerns, especially cavalry movies, and because it starred Charlton Heston, Richard Harris, and James Coburn. But I went with an eye on the credits.

With the exception of my future wife, who more or less had to go to movies if she was going to be with me, I could convince no one they should see this movie. Westerns were much too primitive for them. They preferred things like *David and Lisa* and *Lord of the Flies*. Yet such movies were truly primitive in every sense—formally, intellectually, emotionally.

Major Dundee, on the other hand, in spite of its producers and its musical score, was anything but primitive: its characters had histories, its communities had deep fears and deeper divisions, youth was not exalted but required to grow up. It contained obsession and compromising bargains and stupidity and loss and hatred. You saw how two men, once friends, could hate each other and still risk death together, how a leader's obsession could sweep a whole group along with him, how an outsider's cynicism could coexist with loyalty, how men could be bullied into a unit, fight together, come apart, and fight together again even though their eyes told you the fight was meaningless. I was enthralled. And when they reached their last battle at their last river, and the French were turning for another charge, and the troop was being decimated, and Dundee formed them again while Tyreen tipped his hat and said, "Well, Major, I shall see you in Texas," the movie lifted me to a plane of pure wonder. I am ready to admit that I am perhaps too fond of such moments, but how anyone could resist this was beyond me.

It was also hard to miss, as far as I was concerned, the exhilaration and intelligence of the filming. Here was a director who knew how to place and develop a whole spectrum of characters, how to use the wide screen for composition, how to choreograph a scene and how to heighten its effects. This was most evident in the battle scenes but it was also clear, for example, in the tense confrontation over Hadley's desertion. The scene, as written, is fine in itself; but it's the filming that brings out all the tension (not by calling attention to the camera but by serving the development taking place in the scene). Peckinpah, by the attention he gave to character, background, detail, and movement, had given his work, by cinematic means, the kind of texture a good novel has. And he had shown his ability and predilection for depicting human passions. The characters were not paralyzed by the formulas of the genre nor were they retreating into aesthetic reticence, destroying both genre and life. Though *Dundee* was finally a bit unfinished and remained, with Dundee's return to Texas, a bit too traditionally victorious, it still reached through its traditional form to touch larger issues and realities.

So I remembered Peckinpah's name, as I remembered the names of other directors, as one to look for in the credits. But it was my next encounter with his work that drew me completely under his spell.

Without knowing it was Peckinpah's until it was over, I caught his earlier film, *Ride the High Country*, on late-night television. (Because of his use of the wide screen, especially in crucial, large-scale action sequences, television is unable to do justice to Peckinpah. In fact, his compositions are so fitted to the wide screen that this shortcoming of the medium becomes absolutely clear, something that doesn't happen with every cinemascope movie.)

My attention was captured in the first scene by two things: first, the slight hint of surrealism with its cars, carnival, and camel race, which both stretched the Western (present not only in generic form but in the persons of its stars, Joel McCrea and Randolph Scott) and signaled the awareness of a different, clashing social order; and, second, the alienation of both character and audience as Steve Judd, McCrea's character, thinks the crowd is cheering him as he rides into town and the viewer is not really sure what is happening.

Both the surrealism and the alienation will remain present in Peckinpah's work, growing more pronounced and bitter, until they are forced upon *The Osterman Weekend* as the principal meaning of both the film and the experience of watching it. But here they are mild and used only as a dramatic and qualifying introduction to a pure tale of the search for self-respect and salvation in a world that is alternately too polite, too sordid, or too obsessed to make that search an easy one.

In *Ride the High Country*, character, structure, and theme blend effortlessly, so that even the romantic subplot cannot really be called a subplot because it precipitates not only the climax but the major reconciliations and also deepens the Steve

Judd character. But the purity and simplicity of the film are also due to that character's fight to regain and hold his self-respect through honesty and duty, a fight that is both personal, religious, and social. That is, Steve Judd—like the heroes of Homer and the heroines of Jane Austen—is seeking his values within the roles his society offers and within a certain vision of the meaning of life on earth.

Jane Austen may be the last artist anyone would think of comparing to Sam Peckinpah. But she expresses an imaginative vision in which the individuals cannot simply do whatever they want because they *need* society to do what they want, to be who they are. Alasdair MacIntrye, in *After Virtue*, claims Austen was the last imaginative artist to present such a vision, in which people found meaning and honor and wrestled with choices not by breaking out or retreating from their societies but by filling their roles in those societies with the devotion they were meant to have. MacIntyre's point is that this vanishes from art because of larger cultural shifts and confusions, and it's easy to see his point if one thinks of major modern artists and how often themes of escape, rescue, departure, or renunciation serve as foci for the honorable or devoted life.

Now, one might object to MacIntyre that, whatever the lapses of the great, alienated modern masters, this sort of thing is alive and well in polite fiction, detective fiction, or genres like the Western. Still, it is rare for such works to rise to the level of greatness and reach to the heart of their societies. And, moreover, this link of the social and the personal is not guaranteed by a genre, as one can see from many Westerns, and the issue of personal destiny and social fulfillment is not always grasped or stretched.

But it is in Peckinpah. *Ride the High Country* is a perfect expression of this sort of vision. *Major Dundee* may not be completely (because of Dundee's obsession), but *The Wild Bunch* and *The Ballad of Cable Hogue* still depend on it essentially; what you see in them is that vision being stretched to the breaking point, because of both social change and human passion. In a sense, *Pat Garrett and Billy the Kid* is the requiem for this vision's hold over Peckinpah, while his other films depict protagonists either leaving their roles or writhing in them (or, as in *Junior Bonner*, seeing them shrink to anachronisms).

What saves Peckinpah's Westerns from being merely generic and makes them great imaginative works that happen to have Western settings is that this vision is so real to him and that he is so alive to the forces working against it. As he develops (one might add, as he fights the battles he fights and the U.S. develops as it does in the seventies), he does not retreat into elegy or anachronism but moves in other directions.

As I said, the purity of *Ride the High Country* comes from the presence and clear grasp of this vision. But its force and power come from the perception of other contexts, economic and religious, and from the desperation of the aging Steve Judd. In fact, age, economic life, and religious principle all meet in Judd, making him the rich character he is. Judd's religious principles are not that different from those of the tormented, obsessed farmer Knudsen; but Judd has both experience of life (which makes those principles harder to apply but more deeply grounded) and the gift of compassion, a prime virtue that rigorous Christians would rather ignore.

When I first saw this movie (and then realized it was by Peckinpah), I thought the blend of these elements was so unusual and so effective that I could hardly wait to see what he would do next. My imagination was linked to his.

But the next film took a few years to emerge. Peckinpah began having his problems with producers and studios. Even when the film did emerge, it was cut down from its original length. But for those who saw it and were capable of seeing what was on the screen, it was clearly a masterpiece, the only question being how high to rank it in the history of the cinema, the history of narrative art. It was, of course, *The Wild Bunch*.

In itself, this story of an outlaw gang's botched bank robbery, their agreement to steal guns for a Mexican general, and their suicidal attack on the general's army to rescue a young member of their gang would seem to amount to little more than a sordid, minor Western tale. But what happens on the screen is an explosion of passion and technique, blended perfectly in a vision that is both harsh and compassionate.

The Wild Bunch is actually a very measured film, carefully and classically crafted. It achieves its wonder by its form. There is violence that is gripping not because of graphic images but because it touches fear and sacrifice and because it is filmed to show its pain and its amoral beauty. We see its attraction and we see its destruction; neither is hidden from us. There is tension that grows out of shared pasts, sour memories, degrading alliances, stupid mistakes. There is ambiguity that comes from the obvious savagery of the gang and the equally obvious qualities of courage, guilt, and loyalty they possess and are possessed by.

The battles are stunning, of course, because so carefully choreographed and shot, and because each one is not simply a blazing away but has internal developments that bring out or resolve tensions in the characters. But the other scenes are just as rich, just as carefully done.

The edge of the movie comes from its exploitation of its ambiguities. The viewer is never allowed to rest in easy judgement but is made to see a wrestling with moral choices by people not particularly moral in a very confused and compromised world. These outlaws are hardly romanticized into darling children, society's scapegoats (as in *Bonnie and Clyde* or *Butch Cassidy and the Sundance Kid*), but they are not thereby dismissed as moral agents either. These compromised men, capable of viciousness, are still faced with choices that could salvage or destroy them, choices that involve mortal peril and combat with the communities enclosing them. *The Wild Bunch* was an unusually powerful, unusually complex statement of ambiguity and of honor won in the face of ambiguity. For a popular artwork of that time, it was amazing. (But then, Peckinpah's imagination was not nurtured solely by 'adventure' movies or serials but by artists like Tennessee Williams and Brecht. Indeed, when his later producers complained that all they wanted from him was a "Sam Peckinpah adventure film," one has to wonder just which of his films they would describe as being about 'adventure'.)

Still, one must avoid writing about such a creation as though one were a philosopher or a preacher. The greatness of an artwork lies at a more silent level. To describe it, you would have to tell why one man falling from a roof or a horse, one man sitting on a train, one man looking bitter, one man dying, one man laughing is so much more beautiful and moving than another man doing the same thing in another work. That such a difference of quality in images exists is clear. After it's perceived, one may be able to point to certain things. And yet to say that an image is valuable because of a certain line, a certain light, or a certain arrangement is only to relocate the mystery, not to solve it. And one has still not approached the dialogue, the rhythm of the editing, the blending of themes in the structure. But in a visual art form, these things are not separate elements: they rise from and return to the physical beauty and grace of the moving images. In *The Wild Bunch*, men fall, laugh, and die as they do in few other works.

Perhaps because they do, they release values and meanings that seem to lie dormant in martial imagery and become metaphors for the embattled and questing spirit. Obviously, stories of war and conflict have an appeal far beyond actual battles and brawls. They offer a kind of natural symbolism for all the terrors and conflicts of life. There seems to be a part of the human soul where aspiration and combat are forever mixed that needs such imagery. Anything else would be too mild. Even religious doctrines that verge on total passivity gain in expression by recourse to such imagery, as when St. Paul advises the Ephesians in a famous, detailed passage to "put on the armor of God."

From a purely stylistic point of view, what set Peckinpah's battles apart was his use of slow motion. This appeared in *The Wild Bunch*, though it apparently had been removed from *Major Dundee*, and it continued to mark his style in his subsequent films. (For a detailed and penetrating discussion of the value of slow motion, as well as a brilliant analysis of all the Westerns, one should read Paul Seydor's *Peckinpah: The Western Films*.) As I said above, Peckinpah's battles are powerful precisely because they were *not* mere battles, action sequences, adventures, but rather explosions, resolutions and complication of characters and conflicts. They are where conflicts begin or end, where characters are tested, fulfilled, or destroyed.

The brief slow-motion cuts that became so much of Peckinpah's style contributed immensely to the intensity of his sequences. But they were far more than a mannerism or technique. Many films used and still use slow motion for a lengthening and intensifying effect, especially in action sequences, especially for central characters. But the use Peckinpah made of it remains different, primarily because he adopted it not because it was an available technique but because it answered the needs of his art.

This can clearly be seen from a consideration of the final confrontation in *Ride the High Country*. The shoot-out between Gil and Steve on the one side and the Hammond brothers on the other is so central, narratively and thematically, that it has to be forceful enough and sustained enough to complete all the lines of meaning it is bringing together; but it is only a straight stand-up fight that will be over when half a dozen bullets are fired and most or all the combatants die an uninteresting death; therefore, a way must be found to make the event and its images intense enough to do what is asked of them. The classical adventure film would have either ignored the problem or simply made the action more complex (as in Ford's *My Darling Clementine*). Its modern counterpart would move the complexity into the act of death itself, making it as gory and outrageous as possible (a solution opted for as early as the last combat in the Robert Taylor *Ivanhoe*). But either of these would have marred the purity of this confrontation and subtly shifted the meaning of it, the one making it more devious, the other more brutal. What Peckinpah needs is a way to slow the sequence down. He needs a distortion of time to embody the meaning.

In that film, he solved the problem by montage. From *The Wild Bunch* on, slow motion was to provide the solution. And, of course, it did more than slow the sequence down. It also pulled the audience in and out of the violence. It introduced a mesmerizing rhythm into the sequence as a whole, because the slow-motion shots were used sparingly and briefly. And it allowed the creation of linkages between separate parts of the action, allowing different perspectives and incidents to develop independently but holding them before the audience because of the alternating speeds.

Each of the great Peckinpah battles is a minor story in itself. Not only are the images striking, the sequences built up by the careful isolation of developments, and the action punctuated by peripheral images, but the overall settings and the destinies of the principal characters are always clear and dynamic. It is hard to think of another director whose handling of groups, in or out of action, is more detailed and clear than Peckinpah's is here. His use of slow motion, as of every other technical device, is in the service of a clear conception of the story-within-a-story that such sequences are.

Another element dictating the shape of these battles was the shifting of perspectives integral to Peckinpah's vision. People are in collision because their needs, their desires, their ideals and their pasts are in collision. *The Wild Bunch* gained its reputation from its battles, but they were only the climactic moments of the tense narrative and complex conception that held them. They were in no sense an exercise in terror or savagery or violence for its own sake. They only became as intense and stunning as they were because they were about more than themselves.

Viewing *The Wild Bunch* again recently, I was struck by how measured the ending was. I'm not sure I appreciated this at the time. In the quiet after the death of Pike, I was as exhausted and immobile as any survivor. But the film steadies itself, returns to the bounty hunters, the shattered army and village, the rebels, Sykes and Thornton, and finally the Bunch itself, in happier days.

It was simply an amazing achievement and watching it was

an amazing experience—exhilarating, disturbing, unnerving, inspiring. The film was for me an emblem of imagination and devotion that I carried into the Nixon years and the sourness of America in the seventies.

And it sealed Peckinpah's fame, in more than one sense. Most obviously, and most positively, this film established him as a major artist. He was a recognized partner in society's conversation. If people couldn't take him, they at least knew he was there. And there was enough positive critical fallout to ensure that he was there as a serious artistic presence. As I waited for the next creation, others waited with me.

One can see, looking back, that the achievement of *The Wild Bunch* was so high and became so notorious that it circumscribed all some people knew or wanted to know of Peckinpah. The modern memory is short at best. And being definitively labeled as the creator of one masterpiece (or even one lesser work) is a problem common to many artists. But it was unfortunate that the masterpiece in question was (a) violent and (b) a Western. This tended to limit people's responses and narrow Peckinpah's own options.

Nevertheless, at the time, he could proceed with some achievement and recognition behind him and I could look forward to his films appearing at regular intervals. The next three films remain at a high level of achievement: *The Ballad of Cable Hogue*, *Straw Dogs*, and *Junior Bonner*, forming with *The Wild Bunch* and *Ride the High Country* the core of his work, films in which he was able to explore his vision with relative freedom and in relatively close dialogue with the culture around him. Those three films are smaller in scale. Only in *Pat Garrett and Billy the Kid* and, later, in *Cross of Iron*, would his canvas be as large as in *The Wild Bunch*. And two of them have (with important qualifications) contemporary settings. But they are not as alienated as the other modern films would be.

Coming after *The Wild Bunch*, *The Ballad of Cable Hogue*

was a quiet, bittersweet film and formed an odd, idyllic companion piece to the preceding work. It's the story of one abandoned man who looks for water, wealth, romance, friendship, and a revenge he cannot finally take, and who dies as an accidental victim of progress. Cranky and weathered, Cable was another hero heavy with experience. To get what he wanted, he had to be hard and shrewd. His efforts at domestic life and friendship were sabotaged by his own orneriness.

There was nothing overwhelming about this movie. Its value was in Cable's mistakes, his inability to live in easy harmony and his equal inability to execute an easy revenge. The film was about the vagaries of life, the failure of the heart to rest finally anywhere, and the winning, in spite of that, of fragile loyalties and communities. It was a fitting look by the director of *The Wild Bunch* at the world of home and business. And, despite its low-down characters and gross humor, it seemed to me a highly intelligent film, free of the illusions of youth and harmonious vision.

I've only seen *Cable Hogue* once but I remember being delighted by this shift of subject matter. In later years, when I would hear critics talk about a Peckinpah film ending with "the inevitable bloodbath," I could only marvel at their ignorance. As a general point, the real tragedy of bloodbaths is that they are not inevitable and yet that they still occur, becoming inevitable in certain circumstances. More tragic still, they are not precipitated only by the irrational drives of complete maniacs—but sometimes by cold choices, sometimes by desperate but honorable choices. Such truths were surely central to Peckinpah's vision. But they don't appear in *Cable Hogue*, whose ending must be one of the most beautiful and moving on film (moving, without descending into sentimentality for a moment). The preacher's sermon continues unbroken from Cable's deathbed to his grave to the departure of the mourners as the film simply leaves visual continuity behind and etches a tribute to mutual respect in an imperfect world.

(Perhaps no one can be blamed for being ignorant of this film. When it came out, the only place I found it playing was a drive-in, never a great setting for viewing a picture, and surely a bearer of unfortunate connotations for the opening of any serious film. This is one of those facts of movie distribution that one scarcely knows how to comment on: that, living in a university community with many theaters, I had to see this film by this director, at this stage of his career, in a drive-in.)

Thinking of these films, one was tempted to say that Peckinpah had brought the Western to a new level of quality, giving it unusual aesthetic values and bringing to it a distinctive perspective. Thinking further, one had to notice the obsession with the closing of the frontier and the anachronism of the Western hero. I was eager to see what Peckinpah would do with a modern subject.

But I was missing something. I had underestimated the need Peckinpah had for an idealized past and how much the framework of such a past contributed to the universe of his work. I had also underestimated how decisive for him was the moment his heroes were suspended at: the moment when change was upon them but the past was still real enough to give space and structure to their action. This gave his works both their richness and their intensity. And, like any serious mythology or theology, this framework of a vanished world was an implicit critique both of what passed for social vision at the time and of the times themselves. Nothing he would ever produce that dealt with the modern world would have the grace and freedom of those early works. Looking back, one could see there was no reason to expect otherwise. The shift from his Westerns to his modern films was almost like the shift Thomas Hobbes might see from a social contract back to a state of nature. Possibilities disappear. Conflicts intensify to the purity of absoluteness and abstraction. When Peckinpah turned to the modern world, he didn't keep depending on the cavalry or the community in different costumes, as Ford did. After all, he had never done that in the first place. It is no accident, even given the communal nature of filmmaking and the facts of script availability, that he came up with something like *Straw Dogs*.

There was no problem with the availability of this film. Moreover, with or without having seen it, everyone had an opinion about it and it was discussed as though it were a new, radical philosophy text. I recall the word 'atavistic' being used about it. For many people, *Straw Dogs* and Kubrick's *A Clockwork Orange* become the conclusive evidence that there was a limit to what artists ought to do with violence, difficult to draw perhaps, but clearly crossed in those cases. *A Clockwork Orange* seems to me the more brutal and nihilistic of the two and the respect it has sometimes been shown has always bewildered me. Of course, it has a classy surface, parodies behaviorism, and pours out classical music. Thus it seems a more knowing and subtle creation. And it is a very clever and interesting film. But if one is going to debate human nature on the basis of these two films, the vision of a decent, hesitant man driven to savagery in a hopeless situation strikes me as less cynical and atavistic than the brutal gangs, brutal society, and manipulative scientists of Kubrick's vision.

Nevertheless, there is no arguing away the savagery. I remember sitting in the theater with a large crowd, growing quieter and quieter during the last forty minutes. Then, when the film ended, staring at the screen, until a few heads began turning to look at their friends as though to ask: What have we just seen?

On rare occasions, I have been in crowds that clapped or cheered after a movie. But that stunned silence in the aftermath of *Straw Dogs* is the most eloquent tribute to artistic power I have ever witnessed.

The film remains indigestible because the conflict in it is absolute, and because it is a real conflict. It isn't a story about different gangs of brutes with different methods of attack. The novel it comes from could be called atavistic, but the film does not show the professor being reduced to savagery but being forced to choose a savage battle because of a whole network of values, some of which have helped place him in a vulnerable position—being forced to choose between those values, not reject all of them for the sake of irresistible primitive urges. And when David feels both confused and determined, then both sickened and exhilarated, he is not an ideological cipher in a brute's argument, he is only a realistic character in a situation where order has dissolved. And it is the clear grasp of this character that makes the film so disturbing. The film isn't an ambivalent portrayal of violence. The film is a clear portrayal of the creative and destructive ambivalence of human nature in a chaotic encounter, and a clear portrayal of the dynamics of moral choice among shrinking possibilities.

Of all Peckinpah's work, *Straw Dogs* is the closest to parable or allegory. Yet not because the people and events are ciphers but because the conflicts, under pressure, are pushed to an almost abstract purity. The story, set in a rural community where such things are easily noticed, offers a microcosm of civilization: church, law, business, the struggle for employment, family life (in memory, bonds of honor, twisted loyalties) and—in David, the university mathematician (note the early jokes on this)—a high intellectual culture. The story could be said to demonstrate how easily this shell of civilized life can be cracked and shattered. What saves it from being mere demonstration is the particularity of the events that force the battle: old romances, recent violations, domestic quarrels, community suspicion, brooding hatreds and rivalries, foolish children, violent pranks. These events lead these particular people to a bloody collision, but they are particular, various, not inevitably deadly. Civilized life *is* easily shattered. For the most part, however, it has its power, even over the brutes that finally attack Trencher's farm. What we see is not an essay about the truth of an abstract human nature but a depiction of the loss, under pressure of circumstances, of the restraints of social life. This is a possibility of human life, flowing from a truth about human nature, but it is not a simple truth, nor does the movie portray it as such. In the early scenes, the quiet, obsequious voices of the workers are part of them; thus, when they become whining, hysterical, and belligerent in their attack, they are not merely dropping masks, they are losing control—a control that was real, however fragile, and that allowed them earlier to be repulsed by words.

The point cannot be too much insisted upon: the film is not tearing a veil for us; it is showing how the veil tears for them, and then for us. (It is interesting to note here, too, the discussion over the magistrate's body in which the gang feels driven further because now implicated in murder. At that point, the law appears to them as a palpable boundary.) Moreover, and this too should be insisted upon: the veil is not torn from David, revealing him as at bottom a primitive. He fights back, eventually with equal savagery, but he chooses to fight to save Miles and only after the magistrate is killed. He is sickened after he sees blood, again after he uses the poker. And his peace and satisfaction after the last death are only a sign of humanity's implication in an imperfect world. The only alternatives would be further disgust or a traditionally cinematic grim and stalwart summing up. But the range of his reactions is what is most authentically and disturbingly human about him.

Straw Dogs came to be discussed in terms of anthropological theories current at the time. Anthropology was thus understood as the study of primitive behavior and, thus, of the foundation of all human behavior. But if we take anthropology in the broad sense of the study of humanity, then the film does touch and test us at the edges of our anthropological—and one might even say: theological—assumptions. It is difficult to admit that we would be driven to such a fight. It is difficult to admit that a Good Samaritan would be compelled to defend the victim he finds by choosing such a fight. And it is difficult to admit the savage nature of such a fight. (Even at this date, it is the rare combat memoir that will be explicit about the disgust and the excitement that are mixed in brutal combat. In those that are, shame and pride cannot easily be separated.) The film does raise questions about how we see life and how much we expect from life. It raises them powerfully because it shows both the power and the fragility of civilizing forces. It raises them disturbingly because the human reactions it portrays follow neither a cynical nor an idealistic pattern. They remain human, various, unpredictable. Moreover, it raises them by not blinking at how awful, how tempting, how exciting violence can become.

And here the director is the source of the power. Peckinpah's judicious camera can underscore the brewing tension of a domestic argument or catch the moment of explosion. The violent scenes are vivid and erotic. Yet shot for shot there is less gore in this film than in many others (much less than in most others with similar themes). But Peckinpah catches us up in the savagery, depending less on gore and visual shocks than on the steady drawing out of tension and the ecstatic eruption of battle.

The terms of the story had obviously released something in

Peckinpah himself. In a sense, the elements provide him with a kind of ultimate frontier: isolation, jealousy, cultural incomprehension, attack. Because the terms become so absolute, there is a narrowing of focus in this film, a narrowing that marks all his films with modern settings. Apart from the moment of violence, the setting is claustrophobic. People are blocked, unable to breathe. If one thinks of the housing developments in *Junior Bonner*, the trap of the garbage truck in *The Getaway*, the stench of Alfredo Garcia's head, the darkness and crippling wounds of *The Killer Elite*, and almost anything in *The Osterman Weekend*, it is hard not to conclude that claustrophobia is for Peckinpah a metaphor of modern life. And for the first time he is dealing with a protagonist whose role in his society has gone beyond anachronism: strictly speaking, he isn't an anachronism, but in his immediate community David has no role at all; in fact, he must leave much of his identity behind if he is to act effectively.

Again, this is simply the given story and yet it is also more than that: it taps Peckinpah's own response to modern life, a response that is both an accurate reflection of that life and a personal struggle. (After this, only the sour Pat Garrett will really embark on a more than personal quest through a public identity, and that will be severely compromised from the start.) What touched Peckinpah in *Straw Dogs* and was to mark his response to modern subjects was the narrowing of space, the shrinking of possibilities, the alienation from community.

If *The Wild Bunch* sealed Peckinpah's art for some people, *Straw Dogs* sank it. It was about this time that I started getting into arguments when I championed his work. He was said to 'like' violence. I was accused of 'liking' violence. (If one is looking for primitive categories, think of a few of the elements of life, a few of the possible responses to them, and ask yourself: like or dislike?) Here was a whole nation that officially 'disliked' violence while it was waging one of the dirtier wars of its history with some of the most obscene weapons and tactics.

I will admit, however, that it was about this time that I started to wonder about myself. I felt, with *Straw Dogs*, that I had been taken to the edge of something I wasn't sure I wanted to cross. Again, if I'd been more attentive or perceptive, I would have realized that for Peckinpah it was precisely the edge that was important. Short of the edge was blindness, over the edge was blindness of another sort.

And I will admit I was (pleasantly) surprised by his next film, *Junior Bonner*, a film that those who knew only *The Wild Bunch* and *Straw Dogs* could never have predicted. But it's interesting to note that here again, where there is a change of subject matter, there is only a steady development of theme and technique. One of the remarkable things about Peckinpah's career is how unified it was.

Since I had even less interest in rodeos than I had in rapists, the main interest of *Junior Bonner* for me was what Peckinpah would do with a mild, modern, relatively domestic subject. Even though the mildness of the movie was surprising, what Peckinpah did with it was not. The effect is of a man tidying up. In a sense, this film completes the center of his work and completes, by dwelling on its sunnier aspects and remaining possibilities, his portrait of the kind of heroic personality he (and the traditions he worked in) was drawn to. It can no longer be termed heroic. As the early heroes were out of place, so too is Junior. One is tempted to say that for Peckinpah this sort of person is always anachronistic, out of time, simply because they are heroic, idealistic, graceful. The modern age is thus like every age—but, perhaps because we live in it, more so. What we see in *Junior Bonner* is the celebration of an anachronistic choice: the refusal to adapt, the insistence on the individual's own terms, the refusal of domestic compromise, the turning of a personal quest into mass entertainment. (Some of these themes would be bitterly reprised in *Pat Garrett and Billy the Kid*. Some would be parodied in *The Osterman Weekend*. The last, in my opinion, would befall Peckinpah himself in *The Getaway*.) This is all stated very mildly in this film, but there is really no need for Junior in his society and, like David in *Straw Dogs*, there is really no space for him.

Here the claustrophobia of modern life begins to be explicit in Peckinpah's work. The most intense scene in the movie is Junior's return to his father's cabin just at the moment it is being destroyed, along with the entire landscape, by his brother's cheap housing development. The despair here is more rueful than agonized, perhaps because its agents are not war or brutality but only mediocrity and cupidity. Yet the scene gets all the attention of a Peckinpah battle. It's the heart of Junior's dilemma, what drives and threatens him, the force that is pushing him aside and the life that is making him treasure what he has left. We see one man's visit to an abandoned cabin and his departure as it is bulldozed. But the multiple angles, McQueen's wordless exploration as he handles the objects, the slow-motion cuts, and the marvelously anachronistic shots of the undisturbed cabin appearing after it has collapsed, produce by a master's film style a carefully built sequence of homecoming, yearning, filial respect, loss, and resignation.

But for all its pleasantness, when set against the rest of Peckinpah's work the film seems just this side of collapse or capitulation. Not that it lacks skill. It lacks passion. It's a kind of sunset, despite the songs and despite Junior's driving off into a real sunset—indeed, because of that. (At least he drove off alone.) Junior is simply too happy-go-lucky and at peace with himself. He is aware of the tensions of his world but he's willing to live with them.

It makes for a quiet, private film. The scene in which Junior tells Ace he's broke, the wild-cow milking, the intercut scenes of riders falling in parallel defeats are all masterfully done. And because of Junior's resignation, it does seem like a kind of summing up, a noting of differences, a tallying of losses, a show of anger, but finally a kind of peace.

It seemed to me that Peckinpah had reached a plateau with *Junior Bonner*. What he might do next seemed even more mysterious. He could simply repeat himself. Or, leaving his themes completely and taking only his technique, he could just make any movies that happened to come along. Looking back, this film seems even more of a summing up than it did at the time, a quiet resolution after a furious symphony. Soon he would produce films with all the rage, passion, and cynicism that *Junior Bonner* lacked. But, first, apparently afflicted with the rueful resignation of his last hero, he turned his quest into mass entertainment and made *The Getaway*.

And I enjoyed *The Getaway*. Al-most everyone enjoyed T*he Getaway*. It is a beautifully photo-graphed, well-edited film with an attractive hero and heroine, narrow escapes, clever stratagems, and crisp action sequences. Peckinpah's touch is there in image after image, scenes of tension and scenes of struggle. It's vivid and exciting. And the sleazy deals, physical clutter, and omnipresent garbage of urban life (culminating in the garbage truck scene) add up to a respectable subtext.

But there's something mechanical and slick about it. Though it begins promisingly, with the tedium of prison life priming Doc McCoy for an explosion, Doc McCoy never explodes. He and his wife (his wife!) get away. More than that: they ride off to Mexico in what is probably the only generic Western ending Peckinpah put on one of his major films. Their escape to happiness and Mexico—young, rich, and free—is apparently meant to be taken seriously. Not for the first nor the last time did I sit in a theater amazed by a Peckinpah finale. But this time I was amazed at how awful and trite it was.

It was no wonder that this Peckinpah film was popular. The protagonists really were ciphers, lovable outlaws, and they really got away, with no strings, no ghosts, and only negligible wounds. The police were faceless, as befits the police in a lovable outlaw film. And the villains were not only outlaws without honor, they were old, unattractive, and overweight. It was as though Peckinpah had given in at one stroke to his society's and his own worst impulses and cheapest fantasies.

The failure of *The Getaway* is worth exploring because, coming after the resolution of *Junior Bonner*, it provides a key to what happens next. And it can only do this because *The Getaway* was a project Peckinpah wanted to do, from a novel he knew and admired. One glimpses in his choices the tensions he had reached in his own work and the difficulties he faced, as a creative artist, in turning to contemporary subjects.

If one goes back to Jim Thompson's novel, one is stunned and bewildered by the changes made by the screenplay. I hadn't bothered to read the novel at the time, assuming it was only a cheap adventure story that filming would do nothing but improve. When I finally read it, I found it to be a dark and hair-raising thriller, undistinguished as literature, perhaps, but a powerful gothic tale with brilliant eerie moments. Doc McCoy is no clean professional. He's a sadistic killer from the opening paragraph on. There are scenes of claustrophobic terror in a tiny cave that make the dangers of the movie look ludicrous. And Thompson's fantastic ending in a Mexican kingdom of crime, where the McCoys willingly sell each other out, pulls the rug out from under any illusions about what getting away is like. As I read it, I caught myself thinking: Peckinpah could film this and turn it into a great movie. But he had, and it wasn't.

Since Walter Hill worked on the script, one might be tempted to say that this was simply an instance of the writer triumphing over the director. Indeed, Doc McCoy as he is in the film has much in common with the untouched and almost untouchable heroes Hill has shaped as writer and director. There's the coolness, the professionalism, the orderliness, the absence of terrors and doubts.

But something deeper was going on in *The Getaway*. Mere writers had never stopped Peckinpah before, nor would they in the future. The film's surface is so smooth here because Peckinpah is at no point fighting with the script. One might put it this way: McCoy is another Peckinpah hero, emerging when there is nothing left to say about that hero. Better still: McCoy is another Peckinpah hero, but so much more needs to be said about that hero that saying it would destroy him—therefore, nothing can be said. Or one might say: Peckinpah is shifting eras but, losing historical distance, he loses moral focus and the film becomes more conventionally Western than his Westerns. Or perhaps: Peckinpah's alienation from modern life has grown faster than his ability to express it; *The Getaway* is not by an artist probing alienation but by an artist suffering from it.

For it is an alienated film, hiding behind its craftsmanship. McCoy's bland, clean, untroubled character reveals this. There is scarcely another major character in a Peckinpah film with so little going on inside him. He has none of the drives, none of the doubts, none of the ambivalence, none of the wildness, none of the troubled self-awareness of the characters that had touched Peckinpah's imagination (and would again touch it). His character is untroubled. His life and work (however marginal in objective terms) is simply a given. He simply goes through the motions, and so does the director.

The director must—or he must change. And he will. *The Getaway* is the sleight of hand that takes place before the change.

Peckinpah had shown that he knew too well the kind of frustration that could ravage a man like McCoy, the kind of regret and desperation that would drive him. He had shown that he knew that killing was not simply a professional matter and that when killers were cool they were contemptible. But he didn't show this in *The Getaway* because he had found himself at a point where more needed to be said and he hadn't found the means or will to say it.

The point is not that he had shown all sides of a theme and was now ready for something else. Rather, the point is that to follow these divided men any further would be to change them, implicate them further in the things that warped them, carry them further from fulfillment and resolution. His own exploration of these characters was luring him further. And so was his shift to contemporary settings. Not only was there no place in the modern world, as he saw it, for a Steve Judd or a Junior Bonner. That lack of place brought its own peculiar suffering, which he had yet to deal with.

Doc McCoy, unlike the members of Bishop's gang, is not a holdover from a wilder past, bearing both the flaws and glories of that past. McCoy is a robber by profession. The difference is immense. McCoy has to be shown either darker (as Thompson shows him) or he has to be sanitized (as Peckinpah and Hill sanitize him). He can't simply undergo a change of costume because the society he lives in is radically different and that is part of who he is. Peckinpah could see this in *The Wild Bunch*, but he refused to see it in *The Getaway* because he didn't know what else to see. The shrinking possibilities of modern life, the clutter, the claustrophobia (all of which do appear in *The Getaway*) and the by now crumbling remains of the past form an entirely new arena, with its own mortal traps. This arena, and the people in it, have to be conceived along different lines.

It was precisely the distance of the Western that had allowed Peckinpah to do this before. Again, any mythic structure of golden age or future kingdom allows a perspective on the present that the present cannot give itself. His period films could seem contemporary because they granted both freedom of vision and a different world of values. Giving up the distance, but looking for the same themes, Peckinpah trapped his creation in its own time warp and cut it off from the creative dialogue with the present that most of his other creations had had.

Thus, this modern gangster story turned into a wooden, old-fashioned Western, with the notable absence of the frontier, the pioneering, the codes of conduct. The ride into the sunset here is a symbol of this, as well as a symbol of the film's artistic failure.

It is extremely interesting that this stock Western ending should appear here in a non-Western. Even more interesting is the fact that such an ending is more likely to appear in one of Peckinpah's non-Western films. In the Westerns, the major characters die or they ride away severely compromised. It is in the modern films that they drive away (or sail away) to a new life or a salvaged life—*Straw Dogs, Junior Bonner, The Getaway, The Killer Elite, Convoy*. Still, only in *The Getaway* is that drive without terror or irony. It is as though Peckinpah feels that nothing can be really settled, given the terms he is dealing with, and so he opts for fantasy. But here it is at its strongest and most escapist for the reasons I have mentioned.

This is more than a matter of personal development, more than a question of an artist needing to think a little more deeply. Peckinpah arrived at the impasse of *The Getaway* not only because of the themes he was pursuing but because of the times he was pursuing them in. Political and cultural realities can unbalance an artist. The paper and pencil, the camera, the brush and canvas, the piano still lie there as instruments, but the vision expands or contracts, flourishes or decays. When I say that

Peckinpah saw modern life as a time of constriction and rotten choices, I mean that this is how he saw the United States of the early seventies. And he was certainly not alone.

I wonder if documentaries or histories will be able to convey the sourness of that time. If the sixties had an apocalyptic sense to them, a sense of new creation, the seventies were their stale aftermath, the dark side of the apocalypse. I knew people for whom the future did not seem to exist, for whom the world had become almost timeless. They went from a timeless moment enjoyed under a rainbow to a timeless moment without hope.

At times, we seemed to be dividing ourselves into two separate species, in a ghastly fulfillment of H. G. Wells's vision of humanity in *The Time Machine*. The more or less brutally cynical, who did the real work of the society, faced the divinely or merely simple, who wanted no part of society.

It seems to me this rotting vision and shrinking of possibilities registered like an earthquake in the popular art of the period. As random examples, I would cite: the Hollywood comedies that used generic material yet were at a loss for satisfactory endings; the concerts of the Rolling Stones; Philip Roth's *My Life as a Man*; anything by Diane Johnson. What seems to me crucial is the prevalence of interminable, unsatisfactory situations, the inability to give shape to satisfying solutions, formal or otherwise.

Some artists, under such circumstances, simply register

hopelessness and confusion (as Edmund Wilson argued Hemingway did in the thirties). Some artists, not always the best, take these things as their explicit themes. But it isn't necessary that artists give us useful words of advice on the issues of the day. Those tend to be at least as silly as anyone else's. Art does its work at a deeper level. For their own sake, artists have to regain their balance by reaching for a new synthesis, something that allows them to remain in touch with their own themes and with the shifting world around them. For our sake, artists not only have to register the shocks of their society but have to shape forms that illuminate those shocks. Again, this is not a question of explicit guidance but of imaginative steadying, of enlightening by images, of inspiring by forms that catch the tensions of the times without being destroyed by them.

Because of his peculiar sensibility, Peckinpah was not one to be mesmerized by any of America's simplistic factions. Nor was he well suited to be a philosophical spokesman for anything. But he was an artist, and one whose characters and themes were ripe for challenge and change.

I don't know what strange promptings or accidents brought him back to the Western at just this time with just the story he had to tell, but the event has something about it of a return to mythic sources and a new birth.

By this, I certainly do not mean that Peckinpah received a new burst of energy or that, going back to the Western, he produced another masterpiece. Not at all. But he did find a new synthesis. Returning to the Western, he found a way to probe more deeply into his protagonists and a way of orientating them toward the pressures he was responding to.

Indeed, it could be argued that, from this point on, his films became more rough-edged, less polished, less complete, more volatile, less concerned with the well-rounding of a tale and more with hints, shadows, bypaths, corners. The irony grows. Surrealism grows. Even presented with a well-rounded story, he can no longer make it; the subplots and subtexts have become too fascinating. What he loses in polish, he gains in passion.

This is not the collapse or decay of technique. The technique is still there, and still dazzling, as in the final battle of *The Killer Elite* or in the relentless, parenthetical violence of *Cross of Iron*. But now the technique serves a different vision, finds its place in a different synthesis. The focus of the shift is the protagonist. Central to this last period are people who find themselves in degrading traps or lives they hate, precisely because of the skills and desires that are their most valued possessions, people who do not or cannot simply drop out because they are too driven or compromised to go anywhere else. One might say: characters like Deke Thornton and Ben Tyreen that once provided Peckinpah with powerful contrasts have now become his central subject. Their common mark is their hopeless implication in the corruption around them, a corruption they can neither accept nor have done with. And their common achievement is to maintain themselves for a time on an even bleaker edge of things, taking whatever revenge, pride, or humor they can. This character emerges first and most fully in the aging Pat Garrett, in *Pat Garrett and Billy the Kid*.

An artistic reorientation of this nature is never immediately apparent. Consciously or not, one expects from artists at least veiled repetitions, at most linear developments. It usually takes time and the perspective of succeeding works for an audience to catch up. Peckinpah's return to the Western evoked expectations of another *Wild Bunch*. This film was clearly something else. Watching it was like approaching someone you thought you recognized and groping in conversation for a decisive clue.

The experience could not help but be unsatisfying, both because of the fiasco of the final cut and the different structure of the film itself. Now, watching it, I admire the sureness, almost the serenity, of the new synthesis.

The film is insistent enough upon its own structure that even an audience with strong preconceptions found itself fastening on different elements. It is a work of breadth and languor, but its universe is strangely constricted. Though it's filled with characters, they hardly group themselves at all but remain odd, independent presences. Scenes are ritualized, sometimes to the point of absurdity, giving it the tone of a stately, distanced comedy. Some of the compositions seem like old Remington sketches. The casting, Bob Dylan's score (which also sometimes borders on absurdity), the episodic sequences, the strange minor figures all nudge the film toward surrealism. People rattle on with endless stories. Peckinpah himself appears as a coffin maker. No one seems capable of decision, and no decision seems worth making. No one except Garrett and the businessmen seem to know what they are doing or why, and Garrett hates what he is doing and almost hates why he is doing it. But, finally, it is Garrett who threads all this strangeness together, who at least acts (after a seemingly endless pursuit and search, capped by a maddeningly slow walk), who emerges as the wobbly axis around which this wobbly creation spins.

What only emerged later in articles, interviews, and books was how much was cut out of the film by the studio—how much crucial motivation, how much thematically essential material. (As Paul Seydor says, the only way to 'see' *Pat Garrett and Billy the Kid* is to watch the theatrical version, then watch the longer television version, and finally find some account of the scenes that are in neither, especially the prologue and the epilogue.) The pettiness and venality behind this trashing of a major film would be beyond belief if anything in Hollywood were beyond belief. *Pat Garrett and Billy the Kid* should be remembered as a magnificent, truncated epic—even more so than *Major Dundee*, since that film was not as clearly and brilliantly conceived and integrated as this.

The scope of the story, the character of Garrett, and the very clarity of the themes were the worst casualties of this mindless cutting. (In an eerie way, Peckinpah seemed to be reliving Garrett's story and certainly began to see himself this way, trapped by his skills and reputation in a hopeless charade, working for contemptible men.) If one manages to reconstruct the film in one's mind, one gets a vision of an entire society in motion. We see those who lived its past, those who will make its future, those who are unlucky enough to be caught in the middle. We see the poor, Mexican and American, the merchants, old money, new money, the respectable, the still wild, those who fit and those who don't. That all this is necessary goes without saying. The story isn't only about two friends. It's about two friends in a time of change, with a precise and detailed view of how that time is part of them, inside them, and how it shapes their possibilities and futures. There is determinism here, but it is the artistically valid and immediately felt determinism of particular lives in particular communities. As Romeo and Juliet must die and Lear must be destroyed, so Pat Garrett must kill Billy the Kid. It is Garrett who is the conductor of this vision. And it is Garrett's future, his murder by the same forces that want Billy dead, that vanished when the prologue and the epilogue were removed. These made the entire film into a vision of times past, a vision of loss and futility at the moment of Garrett's death, and made explicit the sense of time and change and the perception of larger forces and strangling contexts that haunt the film. There is no haven in the past and there is no haven from the past. With some sense of what the film could have been, or rather what it actually was before its final cut, one marvels at the artistic victory: all of this hopelessness and disgust so firmly shaped into form, the only form that could hold it and give it a kind of serenity.

The victory here depends on centering the creation on a character who can bear such a weight of guilt, alienation, and perseverance. For a character like Garrett, there is no possible congruence between his values and the options open to him. (This was the plight of Garrett and increasingly the plight of Peckinpah himself. As an artistic development, it was a deepening of Peckinpah's themes and a response to the souring of American society.) A pure action hero is defined only by what he does; but an ironic hero like Garrett can't be. The important things become why he does what he does, how he does it, what forces him to do it, what he won't do. These become the important things because of what is happening around him.

A way of marking this change is to note the different quality of the film's violence. No longer is it ecstatic release or wild collision. Most of it is casual, sometimes pointless, sometimes calculated. Only for Garrett, when he shoots Billy, is it wrenching, and it becomes for him not victory or escape but only one more trap. After Billy falls, Garrett shoots his own reflection in a full-length mirror. But one needs not only the self-destruction of Garrett but his actual murder by the new forces of power to fill out the themes. The personal choice and loss need to be seen as more than personal, as the greater choice and loss of a shifting society.

Pat Garrett and Billy the Kid is the climax of Peckinpah's exploration of the roles available to the people that interest him. The distance between personal quest and social reality can get no greater. But now the work itself bears that knowledge in a form appropriate to it. And it does have a kind of serenity, partly because of the pacing, partly because of the distancing of time, and partly because Peckinpah himself has finally grasped the direction he needed.

In his next film, he was to proceed further in that direction so quickly that almost no one was capable of following. *Bring Me the Head of Alfredo Garcia* came and went so fast that even the handful of people who might have been interested in seeing it scarcely had the chance. Beginning with the title, there was little about it to attract a large audience or to soothe squeamish critics. In the eyes of some people, Peckinpah had at last given in to his lowest urges and allowed his work to fall into the negligible genre of splatter films, where—according to them—it had belonged all the time.

When Pauline Kael reviewed *The Killer Elite* (which she discussed under the title of "The Nihilistic Poetry of Sam Peckinpah"—a step up, perhaps, from the fascism she saw in *Straw Dogs*), she noted that it was impossible to comprehend Peckinpah's recent work at the surface level—one had to see the moods and obsessions beneath the narrative line. Labels aside, her perceptions were, as usual, acute. She noted a groping for different themes, a shifting of obsessions, a turn toward characters who sell themselves but still try to hang on to part of themselves.

This strikes me as exactly right. But the shift was achieved in *Pat Garrett*, and *Alfredo Garcia* is a leap ahead down the same path. When Peckinpah was asked later what he would consider the essential Sam Peckinpah film, he mentioned not the famed masterpieces but *Alfredo Garcia*—a measure, I think, of the rightness he felt in the course he had followed. Kael thought this film still bore the mark of a lack of direction and that Warren Oates was too weak a choice for the protagonist. But I think Oates was chosen precisely because he was a minor figure from earlier Peckinpah films, thus standing for the shift of imaginative interest, and that the film's rough, murky, obsessive structure was not confusion but a deliberate turning away from an audience.

Here was a project that was chosen by Peckinpah, as *The Getaway* was. It was not a question of his being thwarted or having a subject thrust upon him. He was doing precisely what he wanted to do. But in this case he wasn't only suffering from alienation but creating out of his alienation. There is little wonder and a certain fitness in the one film being a commercial success and the other film a failure.

The appearance of Warren Oates was like a self-referential allusion in the work of an obscure poet. With *Alfredo Garcia*, Peckinpah's films became not only more brooding but more private, idiosyncratic. These last films would never get the attention the early films did. There was no way they could: not only were they mood pieces, but their vision was harsher and they were no longer in close dialogue with the audience. Peckinpah and the audience had parted company.

When *Bring Me the Head of Alfredo Garcia* appeared unheralded and unadvertised in my town, I found myself for the first time hesitating about attending a Peckinpah film. Not only was there no longer a question of getting very many people to accompany me, but the new film's title and some early reports of it made me wonder if I wanted to follow Peckinpah any further. One week's hesitation was enough because the film was soon gone and I was left to wait until it reappeared in rerun houses before I could see it.

I remember this hesitation because there was no other film-maker that I followed so avidly, and even at the time I found it strange that I would skip one. But as I recall, my feeling was that our culture had become so sour it could no longer afford any more bitterness. I wanted to draw back from anger and death. I recall telling someone (at a Peter Watkins festival) that if we were seriously opposed to war and interested in healing society we ought to limit ourselves to producing things like *A Midsummer Night's Dream* (as though that were a simple matter of choice, as though that would solve anything).

This feeling didn't last long and the withdrawal behind it was not a very deep response to a rotting society. But I mention it as an example of how one person's sensibility, having been closely wedded to one artist's vision, can part company with that artist's quest when it approaches limits the person would rather draw back from. I was tempted to cease pondering the issues Peckinpah was holding in intolerable tension. In any case, at that time, he and I parted company.

As he had turned from the audience, so I the audience had turned from him. It is perhaps a mark of the hysteria of the times that I felt challenged to attend *Alfredo Garcia*, that I could not get myself to attend, and that having missed it I felt as though I had betrayed something. But, in a sense I had. Artists, once they gain an audience, have the right to expect the attention of that audience. As artists can hardly expect their audience to remain either agreeable or in agreement with them, so neither can the audience expect that from the artists. All either has a right to is the dialogue. But the terms of the dialogue had become too strained and it was breaking down from both sides.

The film begins as the story of a wealthy father who wants the head of the man who dishonored his daughter. The elements of the story are on the one hand melodramatic and on the other hand almost biblical. They echo the family conundrums of the Old Testament and Jesus' parables of the New Testament, which use domestic confrontations to explore issues of identity and ultimate faith. *Alfredo Garcia* begins as a story of tainted honor and retribution. All sorts of dogs are loosed to find Alfredo's head. But Alfredo is already in his grave. And one of the dogs is a down-and-out friend of his who acquires the head from the corpse, then grows fond of it, traveling and conversing with it like a mad Elizabethan character, until he finally slaughters the father and his bodyguards in a hopeless showdown. The final image is of the barrel of a smoking gun.

This is all raw enough but the film lingers in the mind, because of both its images and its themes. It's memorable for its eerie light and dust, the dislocating mixture of technological and pastoral imagery (giving it deliberately its own time warp, but one that works for its themes), touchy sexual encounters, and the strange characters that drift in and out of the episodes.

The fact that Alfredo is already dead when the search begins propels the terms of the story into a bizarre key. We see themes stripped of all reason and context: revenge reaching beyond the grave, loyalty and affection discovered for a severed head, demands of conflicting honor being fought to the death when death has already put Alfredo beyond honor's satisfaction. We see revenge, loyalty, honor, and friendship severed from their normal contexts, almost pure abstractions.

One is first tempted to say the film is an expression of nihilism and disgust. But nihilism doesn't move anyone to face danger and sacrifice. And disgust doesn't move anyone to insist on a point of honor. It would be more accurate to say the film is an expression of various ideals, shattered into isolated qualities and given a purity that borders on madness. Or one could say the film is an expression of the rediscovery and rescue of ideals (in a warped state) from disgust and nihilism.

All of it serves Peckinpah's purpose: here is a demeaning quest, backed by big money. A low-down piano player, grabbing for anything, responds, then finds he can't serve the people he has sold out to, even when it makes no real difference. He finds it makes a difference to him. So he reverses the direction of retribution and takes what revenge he can. Choices may have shrunk to absurdity, but choices still matter. Hopeless endings aren't nihilistic but gestures of desperation and defiance.

By Peckinpah's next film, *The Killer Elite*, I was ready to rejoin his path. His turn toward compromised figures, peripheral figures, people squeezed out but still functioning seemed a more eloquent artistic statement for the times than other creations that were more steady, rounded, serene. And the film itself, on the surface, seemed to move back a little toward the mainstream, with a recognizable espionage setting and a respectable cast (though why its distributors thought it would make a good Christmas movie escapes me).

But, as Kael noted, the surface of *The Killer Elite* is the least important part. The film is not about espionage at all but about what are now Peckinpah's central themes: compromise, betrayal, salvaged honor, personal victories. The ninja assassins that only emerge for the last battle are like the hidden Chinese seamen of *Moby Dick*: they dislocate the cultural references and hurl the work onto a weird level of surrealism.

Again, the structure is constipated because the director is following submerged themes, minor characters, sidelights. The personal scores of the protagonist are settled lamely (when someone else shoots that man who wounded him) and brutally (when he cripples the man who gave the order), but in either case they are settled before the plot's final resolution in a hypnotic battle-ballet, which for both director and protagonist seems nothing but a display of aesthetic skill and delight.

Indeed, that battle of violent grace in pure light, with a random collection of eccentrics fighting a grey, faceless horde aboard the mothball fleet, is a resolution of the imagery and subtext of the film more than of the plot. It scarcely matters that the Asian diplomat is settling something. What matters is that the film's pain and claustrophobia have given way to open air, splendid performance, free movement. There is a shot, between two moments of the attack, of James Caan and Burt Young laughing in ecstasy, that strikes one as the director's cry of self-satisfaction and happiness. And when they sail away together, leaving not only their employers but their personal lives, it is not so much *The Killer Elite* that has found a resolution but the movie that Peckinpah constructed within it.

It is scarcely helpful to explain the film as satire, as Peckinpah did, or to complain, as others did, that the realism is at war with the humor. The film, as Kael argued, simply departs from its own plot. As in *Alfredo Garcia* (but not so well integrated with the surface details), Peckinpah is pursuing fragmented ideals, qualities that have become isolated, and so warped. And yet it is not quite true to say the surface is irrelevant to the themes; as in *The Osterman Weekend*, the betrayals of espionage are metaphors for the betrayals of society at every level. The plot is fueling the themes, but in an oblique way. There can be no satisfactory resolution in the world of the story because the world of the story is part of what the director finds despicable, and stands as a symbol for the rest of it.

As in all his films with contemporary settings, *The Killer*

Elite gives off an air of cheapness and claustrophobia. The world is trivial, cluttered, stifling. But when Mike is crippled, the terms change: the paralysis Peckinpah's characters feel becomes almost literal and, as in *Alfredo Garcia*, what marks Mike is that he is hurt because there were things he did value and trust completely. Ideals are discovered in the midst of disgust. His pain, painful recovery, and permanent disability are given disproportionate weight. Espionage waits; this is Peckinpah's version of ordinary life. And when the violence finally bursts out in the full sunshine of the noon battle, the film seems to become completely abstract, but it's an achievement of clarity: both pledges and skills can be valued and used, even though there is little to connect them to. And here it does join the early masterpieces, even though it has a different, narrower emotional weight: issues aside, at a certain point conflict and performance are demanded, and a certain clarity can be achieved. But nothing comes of it; Mike can only sail away.

Paul Seydor, at the close of his study of the Westerns, compared the art of Peckinpah to that of Norman Mailer. And in *Bring Me the Head of Alfredo Garcia* and *The Killer Elite*, the similarity is striking: as with so much of Mailer's work, the films seem less individual works than pieces from the journal of the same man, detailing a rootless quest. While the sense of the past is part of these films, found in past friendships and old wounds, which give the characters the weight of experience common in Peckinpah films, that sense tends to be narrowly personal. When it is more than that, it is either accidental (past plots which happen to be in motion) or symbolic (the older Mexican culture of *Alfredo Garcia*, the mothball fleet of *The Killer Elite*). They lack the historical scope of the Westerns (not in the sense of period details but of social forces at work). They have the isolation that goes along with alienation but not the view of social conditions that would counterbalance those themes.

Peckinpah had once said that he didn't make Western movies but movies that happened to be set in the West. This was true as far as it went. But, as I noted above, there was something in his vision that needed and benefited from historical distance. It allowed his grasp of social forces to come out and gave his contempt for the present an anchor in history. That this was not simply a yearning for a golden age (however authentic that can be) but an essential part of his artistic sensibility can be seen from *Pat Garrett and Billy the Kid*, in which his developing response to the present undercuts his older themes but does so precisely through a reevaluation of the past and the forces at work in it.

With *Cross of Iron*, he regains this historical perspective in a new setting, the retreat of the German army from the Russians in 1943. It gave him, for the last time, a full canvas to work on and it allowed him to give a further twist to his meditations on individuals and their societies, narrow choices, compromised loyalties, and strangled hopes. (One can only admire a contemporary film director who—if the story is true—rejected both *King Kong* and *Superman* for an opportunity to develop his own obsessions.)

This film seems to me now a lasting and magnificent achievement. By this I don't mean it is easily likable or flawless. Magnificent works of art, though they may be the former are rarely the latter—especially when they deal with extreme situations or powerful and dark passions. But it is an extraordinary use of film and it manages to get Peckinpah's concerns on the screen with a breadth that had been absent since *The Wild Bunch* (not counting what was left out of *Pat Garrett*). *Cross of Iron* bears the same relation to even excellent conventional war films that the poetry of Hopkins bears to that of Tennyson: the imagery is stronger and more sharply defined, the rhythm is both more free and more captivating. The whole work is wound more tightly and exerts a greater pressure on the audience, and there is an insistence that the artist's quest is not mere spectacle but our quest as well.

When I first saw the film, I thought it lacked an ending. (I had read the Willi Heinrich novel on which it was based and I thought it, too, lacked an ending.) I was also bewildered by what I felt were pointless rearrangements of the story made by the script. The second viewing allowed me to get over some of the dis-ease resulting from familiarity with the novel. Though I would still quarrel with some of the script's choices, I now find the film's ending superb. The visual litany of war photographs, ending with a quote from Brecht about the return of tyrants and war, risks reducing the film to the level of an antiwar speech. But it would be hard to reduce this film and its images to anything. And war photographs themselves are always more eloquent than speeches. Moreover, as the photographs are underscored by James Coburn's laughter, growing more ghastly and cynical as the photographs go on, the film remains on the edge of art and moral statement—the far edge, perhaps, but the edge that is seldom missing entirely from great works of art. Both the laughter and the horror flow directly from the bitterness of the film and the ending is simply the ending Peckinpah needs—an ending in tension and challenge, ending not so much on the screen as in the audience's lap. It was an ending Brecht would have liked.

The prologue is almost a parade of Peckinpah themes and devices. Newsreel footage of boys climbing a mountain, accompanied by a children's song, is intercut with footage of the rise of the Nazis, with the song giving way to a military march. The boys are revealed as a Hitler youth group, and the images of war become more stark (even as we see domestic scenes of Hitler himself), while the march and the children's song continue to alternate. Finally, the newsreel footage is intercut with scenes from the movie itself, so that the story of Steiner's platoon seems to arise directly out of the story of the Third Reich (just as the frozen images at the end flow directly into the painful photographs of this war and later wars, including Vietnam). So we see children's fascination with the deadly, the polite façade of a violent society, and the implication of the characters in their society's corruption.

For the American audience at least, there is a further twist in the prologue. With the possible exception of the American Nazi Party, the symbols conjured up in the first few moments (at the beginning of a war film) suggest to most viewers impending catastrophe, conquest, and oppression. Yet, as at the beginning of *The Wild Bunch*, when the polite soldiers are revealed as the outlaws, our sympathies are dislocated slightly as the Nazi emblems introduce and identify the characters we will come to care about. In both films, the dislocation frees us to contemplate the plight of particular people. The difference, however, lies in the different destinies of the characters: *The Wild Bunch* leads us into a reality affirmed by its characters, *Cross of Iron* into a reality the characters themselves are at war with.

So, too, the movement of the prologue from one time period into another was the kind of movement Peckinpah had wanted to give *Pat Garrett and Billy the Kid*. But in that film the prologue would have placed the story in the perspective of Garrett's future. In *Cross of Iron*, the prologue establishes the story's roots in a commonly recognized, tragic past, which the epilogue carries into our present.

Steiner himself, played by James Coburn (who ages Heinrich's hero considerably but connects the film visually to *Pat Garrett*), is simply the late protagonist of Peckinpah: the skilled man who hates his work, the honorable man who is corrupted by his alliances, the uncontrollable avenger who turns on his superiors when he can no longer tolerate their betrayals.

The war gives the film a unity the two preceding films lacked: with its hopeless, seemingly endless retreat, its omnipresent violence, and the clarity of its extreme situations. And it gives Steiner's character a central role in the large drama that surrounds him: he has a role but even less of a future than Pat Garrett had.

The descent of this protagonist to an even bleaker level can be marked by the depiction of violence. As usual, Peckinpah's technique serves his themes: while the violence of his early work could be ecstatic (or, in *Pat Garrett*, casual), here it is simply destructive, constant, unnerving. There has simply been too much of it too long for these men. The constant bombing and machine-gunning, the numerous cuts throughout the film to soldiers falling and dying, seem finally to wrap characters, film, and audience in a deadly, alien environment. (It is probably impossible to convey in print how constantly these short cuts to explosions and death interrupt the film. Perhaps my impression exaggerates their frequency but I found their cumulative effect relentless. This is surely one of the least serene war films ever made.) The set-piece battles are hardly ecstatic, only desperate. When Steiner's platoon (in a fitting touch of surrealism) try to return to their lines in Russian uniforms and are massacred, the use of slow motion underscores not their hardness—as in *The Wild Bunch*—but only their suffering. When the faces of his dead platoon flash through Steiner's mind, the flashbacks again echo the end of *The Wild Bunch*—except that there the faces spoke of moral victory, here only of betrayal and waste. And Steiner's hellish laughter couldn't be more different from the laughter of Old Sykes.

There are magnificent moments and touches: the haunting long shots of Steiner's men in the smoke of no-man's-land; the frantic battle in which Steiner is wounded; Steiner's hallucina-

tions in the hospital; the decent officers stacking papers and dis-
cussing honor during a bombardment (all the more effective
because it isn't played for laughs and because their obvious de-
cency and honor only provoke Steiner's contempt); Captain
Stransky's verbal trapping of his homosexual aide; the reappear-
ance of the dead Russian boy that Steiner had befriended, which
provokes his fit of laughter. And throughout the film there is the
simple but rare achievement of grace and rough beauty in image
after image.

Perhaps the most effective thing about the ending is that
there is no resolution of the battle in progress. In general, there
is nothing easier to resolve than an action film, especially one
dealing with history. After all, all battles end, if only in mutual
exhaustion, and we all know who won this war. But the lack of
resolution is chosen: the battle is endless, the retreat is endless,
the laughter is endless. The choice comes from a Brechtian refusal to allow the work of art to be self-contained. The surrealism and the alienation present in the opening scenes of *Ride the
High Country* have grown in Peckinpah's work to immense pro-
portions.

For all its bitterness, *Cross of Iron* demonstrated—to me, at
least—that Peckinpah, following his own path through difficulties and his own deviousness, had in no sense lost the capacity
to achieve greatness in new directions. As it turned out, neither
of his next two projects offered even the possibility of such an
achievement. And then he died. Whether or not someone like
Peckinpah could have expected to live longer or to find people
who would continue to back him is a real question. As many
people said, the marvel is that he managed to make the films he
did. And yet he did manage that and forged a remarkably consis-
tent body of work within a community that does not make such
things easy. So it seems a pity that he was not given more scope

for his work, especially when one considers the midgets producers routinely squander their money on, with less reward and much less glory.

After *Cross of Iron*, Peckinpah returned to the U.S. to make *Convoy*, a film that bewildered me from its very conception. Why would this director, after fighting to forge his last four harsh and idiosyncratic films, agree to direct a movie based on a hit song about truckers? Perhaps he wanted to try out new material or test his vision in a different context. Perhaps he was only tired of fighting.

At any rate, this was one Peckinpah film I was not even tempted to attend. I have since seen it, but only on television, so I am unable to judge the quality of the compositions. Many people have praised these, going so far as to say the trucks were the real stars of the movie. But I know of no one who has claimed the movie made a great deal of sense, and to say that the machines were handled spectacularly seems a peculiar tribute to pay to this particular artist.

I suppose, if the aging Peckinpah had a lighter side, it could be said to show up here. The film is pleasant enough and has, for the most part, a breezy tone. But raunchy breeziness is hardly in short supply in American movies. And the gripping parts of the film—the jail sequences, Kristofferson crossing the last bridge against a deputy with a machine gun (one of the rare times I would accuse Peckinpah of repeating himself or introducing gratuitous violence)—either pull against the tone or stick out as alien elements. Indeed, most of Peckinpah's themes that are touched in *Convoy* appear almost flippantly, by rote: the obsessive following of an apparently self-defeating plan of action, the alienation, the cynical laughter of the hopeless, the chance alliances. As in *Junior Bonner* (but with much less success) and *The Getaway* (but with much less superficial gloss), Peckinpah displays his themes in contemporary settings with nothing more than tired resignation. And, tellingly, the characters once more ride off in the end, away from their problems.

Convoy makes one reflect again how curious it was that an artist so much in dialogue with his era should carry on that dialogue through period works, and that his contemporary works should either be jagged parables or superficial entertainments. The former, of course, are far more valuable as artistic achievements. And, in *The Osterman Weekend*, Peckinpah would close his career with another contemporary film, but one that would be a fitting successor to *Alfredo Garcia* and *The Killer Elite*.

But before that, there was another long wait. One had grown somewhat used to these, following Peckinpah's career. But age and ill-health and reputation for difficulty began to appear as insurmountable obstacles. If an artist's last creation, justly or not, always has the loudest voice in determining possible options, *Convoy* seemed a disaster indeed—both in terms of critical assessment and mainstream financing. The years went by, Peckinpah had a nearly fatal heart attack, and I wondered if he would ever direct again or if, directing, he would produce something significant.

Watching for his work, by this time, had become for me a creative touchstone. The dialogue with his work was part of my life, for better or for worse. So it was with hope and excitement that I read, in an article about Robert Ludlum, that *The Osterman Weekend* was to go before Sam Peckinpah's cameras.

Out of long habit (and even though I knew this wasn't always the smartest thing to do), I got hold of a copy of the novel. I had never read anything by Ludlum and I found it interesting enough, though rather labored in its opening chapters. But I thought it was the kind of thing Peckinpah could once have polished and deepened, so that the elegance and power of his filming would carry it to a higher level. (One reviewer remarked that the book offered the material to make *Straw Dogs Meets The Killer Elite*.)

So, once again, not knowing it was for the last time, I set myself to watch the movie ads (which was fortunate since the ad campaign was abysmal) and rushed to see it as soon as it came to a nearby theater (which was also fortunate since it left in one week, though it has had a respectable life on cable television).

It isn't hard to understand its failure and early disappearance. It's hardly a piece of slick moviemaking. The musical score seems like random noise. The final rescue would be hard to swallow in a television series. Unless I'm deceived, there are a couple of editing cuts out of place in the action sequences. The climactic scenes offered by Ludlum's novel are avoided, and Ludlum's last twist—that the character played by John Hurt really is a Russian agent—is left out. (Peckinpah was apparently locked into the script and lost some of his touches in the final cut.) For the most part, the film seems cold and rigid. Even what is valuable in it is unpalatable, unsweetened by commercial packaging.

It's also not hard to understand the difficulties of designing an advertising campaign, especially given the morons that usually do this sort of thing and their estimation of what the public can grasp. (Anyway, there seemed to be something in Peckinpah that inspired clumsy advertising.) Much like *The Killer Elite*, *The Osterman Weekend* can scarcely be said to deal with espionage but rather with paranoia, voyeurism, distortions of reality, and the sourness of modern life. It's about the infection of private life by the technology and the games of the powerful. (Seen this way, casual asides in the film underscore the themes neatly, e.g., the televised debate about germ warfare experiments on unsuspecting soldiers that goes on in the background of the opening scenes.)

Ludlum's novel centered on a news commentator named John Tanner who was led by the CIA to believe one or all of his closest friends were Russian agents. In the novel, we see Tanner's friendships destroyed by his suspicion until he realizes that it is Fassett, the CIA agent, who is the real spy. Fassett's story of his own wife's murder was a fabrication, and his CIA superiors had allowed Fassett to bait Tanner so that they could destroy Fassett's network. The book has one of the simpler Ludlum plots but one of his chillier endings: Tanner lives but his entire network of personal relations has been poisoned.

The movie makes several changes in this plot but one is significant: Fassett isn't a Russian agent. Indeed, there are no Russian agents anywhere and, as far as the movie is concerned, Russia itself may be a convenient creation of the CIA. The killing of Fassett's wife (arranged by the CIA) is taken as real and provides the entire occasion for the action. Fassett is out for revenge and he is using Tanner, mercilessly and brutally, to strike back at the CIA. It is otherwise basically the same war of shadows and deceptions, but the values are shifted crucially. Tanner is still used, a victim of appearances. But the CIA puppetmasters are no longer revealed as being in control. No one is in control: the final confrontation is actually a three-sided battle for the control of a television message (concluding brilliantly with an empty moderator's chair). Most importantly, Fassett, though a liar and a killer, has a just cause to plead.

Whether Fassett's character was changed to simplify the plot (and whether that succeeded in improving it) or whether there was a greater purpose at work, the shift had a decisive effect on the plot's allotment of sympathies: against all the logic of the original story, Fassett becomes the engaging protagonist—first, because he is much more active and informed than Tanner, and second, because he is ruthless. The novel was a parable of a victim. The film became a parable of a just but indiscriminate avenger.

The more I see the film, the more I think it orders itself around John Hurt, who plays Fassett. This may be only a matter of interpretation because the wires of sympathy are undoubtedly crossed. But Fassett could not have been better designed on purpose to attract Peckinpah and his themes: he is the skilled professional, betrayed by his own people, using their techniques to take his revenge. Shot after shot has no other purpose but to allow Fassett to comment on the action and take delight in the drama he is creating. Rutger Hauer as Tanner has been criticized for being a stiff cipher. But there is little in the conception of Tanner to draw the director's sympathy, while Fassett is someone he can easily imagine himself being.

And yet these are simply the elements of the story. What is most notable about *The Osterman Weekend* is the experience of watching it. In this film, Peckinpah's assault on the audience becomes total.

By that, I obviously do not mean it is the strongest film he ever made, the most powerful. On the contrary, it may be one of the least compelling. Peckinpah is deliberately working against the audience, assaulting the audience as audience, trying to make it wonder why it is staring at a screen (and why it spends so much of its time before so many screens), making it impossible to forget it is staring at a screen.

When the first frame came on the screen, I wanted to yell "Focus!" Then I decided that the problem wasn't lack of focus but a terrible print. Only when the camera began to pull back did I realize we were watching other people watch a film—as we would be doing for the entire movie: watching them watch others through TV cameras, rewatch old films, rerun them out of sequence, control our attention by multiple screens, until the last scene shows a man answering questions that were asked hours earlier while shots of a helicopter are edited in as though another movie had begun. I found myself mentally noting, over and over again, "this isn't happening." That could sum up Peckinpah's final creative judgement on American life: "none of this is really happening: it's the manipulation of shadows." The way the pursuit of Fassett closes in at the end is a laughable climax to an espionage film, but a wonderful finale to a film about distortions of reality. Our experience of watching movies is used to undercut our experience of watching this movie. The last frame we see is an empty chair in an empty studio—no artist, no audience. (Again, it is no wonder that the chairs on the other side of the screen were empty, too.)

The film is meant to confront us with ourselves as spectators. The sex in it is cold and painful, unlike standard movie sex. It's made more bizarre by our knowledge that someone else is watching the couples but then we realize: so are we. Part of the film is saying "You are putting these things together," part "Here—you put them together." In any case, the unreality is writ large: none of this is happening—not the television scenes we see, not the larger world of the movie. We are in a theater. But we are being told what one artist thinks we are like.

Peckinpah is using form to alienate us but not as it would be used in an experimental film. In earlier works, he had undercut our expectations; here he goes the furthest he ever went in undercutting the experience of watching itself. But his concern is still to lead us into a certain vision. The formal alienation doesn't make the film abstract, it retains an artist's concern with the quality and shape of the totality of experience. This film is not completing or heightening that experience for us, in a classical sense, but dislocating us from it because of a judgement that it is worthless and deceptive. The technique does not come from an interest in experiment but a disgust with glamour, manipulation, deceptive appearance. Tanner's television show is called *Face to Face*, but no one ever appears face to face: only through television hookups.

Peckinpah has a lot of fun with these distortions: the dog's head in the refrigerator (recalling the cat from *Straw Dogs*), which turns out to be a fake; the dog at other moments looking at the camera (Fassett's and ours) like a coy actor; Fassett watching baseball on some of his screens and murder on others; Fassett forced into doing a mock weather report when his equipment backfires.

As in most of Peckinpah's later work, the film is fractured by minor characters and multiple points of view. (Apparently there was more of this in earlier cuts.) There is a scene in which a group of Tanner's friends are trying to escape in an RV: one woman is smearing her face with cocaine and singing "Jesus loves me" as the RV blows up. Her voice completes the song as we watch the explosion. On the surface, the scene is neither necessary nor particularly moving: but what's actually being shown is the director's opinion of American leisure, drugs, and religion. (One might say this is religion's last gasp in Peckinpah's work: from the traditionally rooted compassion of Steve Judd, through the fanatics and temperance marchers, the ineffectual or odd ministers, the peasant cultures, memories of religious training, down to the single stanza of a Sunday School song. Perhaps the distinction is too fine but to one who has grown up in the church the point seems purposeful and well made: "Shall we gather at the river?" is a congregational hymn of communal hope; "Jesus loves me" is a children's song of personal comfort.)

The alienation and the fracturing heighten elements that were always present in Peckinpah's work. So, too, do the claustrophobic elements of the film: people are gassed, trapped in small places, held under water, and are always under surveillance. No one can breathe in this closed, suspicious world.

The Osterman Weekend cannot rank as a great film but it does stay in the mind because it was cunningly made by an odd and cunning artist. And while its poor reception (and the narrowness of the material to begin with) did not hold great promise for Peckinpah's future, his own performance and the presence of his peculiar explorations seemed to offer proof that he was very much alive as an artist and very much in dialogue with the sickness of his culture.

I wish there had been more films from him—not simply other films, rediscovered, to return to but new creative reflections from him, new directions, more of his devious and canny tales. But there wouldn't be. The last fresh Peckinpah image I would ever see was of John Tanner's empty chair, facing a deceived and deceptive audience.

I heard that Peckinpah went on to make a rock video, which seemed to me one step from doing television commercials or drawing an unemployment check. And then I heard that he died.

I had followed his work out of one era of complacency into another. I can still watch it on videocassette but I almost feel guilty doing it, knowing his scorn for the small box, knowing what it does to his compositions. (Imagine seeing the paintings of the world only on art museum postcards —all cropped to the same square size.) I have not lost the creative deposit but I have lost the creative dialogue.

And the commercial paralysis of the cinema today is enough to make me weep. Here we have a magnificent art form, capable of exploring human experience with enormous power and beauty. But those who oversee its production and distribution seem to be gripped by triviality and timidity. I suppose the same could be said of other arts. But books, scores, and canvases are, in some sense, within the means of individual artists and, if buried for a time, remain recoverable. Great cinema requires great investment. And those capable of producing great cinema are not always lucky or tactful enough to attract great investment. Their work, thus, remains not hidden but unmade.

For a time, it seemed as though the icons of our age, the aesthetic foundation of cultural discourse, were and would remain cinematic. The cinema was both accessible and subtle. But the films being made during Peckinpah's last years scarcely bear comparison with the films being made during his early years.

They tell us less about ourselves. They don't try to tell us very much about anything.

Sam Peckinpah, as trapped and ill used as he felt (or made himself out to be), never stopped trying. I honored him when he lived and I lament his passing. He had the artist's gift and the artist's task, the same given by the Lord to Jeremiah:

> See, I have set you this day over nations and over kingdoms, to pluck up and to break down, to destroy and to overthrow, to build and to plant. (Jer 1:10)

To do all this, with only the artist's weapon: imagination; to say "this is so" and "this is not so" and to show the way only by images.

In the life of a people, artists are indispensable. But we don't get the same thing from all of them, nor do we all want what they have to give. They change, we change. And when they die, we the audience simply disperse, like a crowd after a movie, to join other audiences before other visions.

But that intimate dialogue with one particular vision is irreplaceable. That's both the privilege and the tragedy of being a near contemporary of a great artist. The artist's end is the audience's limit. With Peckinpah's death, I was given one of mine. But it was an unforgettable privilege to have seen what he had to show.

www.ingramcontent.com/pod-product-compliance
Lightning Source LLC
LaVergne TN
LVHW021616080426
835510LV00019B/2602